T0243724

Tristan/Yseult

Tristan/Yseult

HARRY BONELLE

UNICORN

First published by Unicorn
an imprint of Unicorn Publishing Group, 2024
Charleston Studio
Meadow Business Centre
Lewes BN8 5RW

www.unicornpublishing.org

ISBN 978-1-911397-90-8

Cover design Felicity Price-Smith
Cover illustration by Vivian Head
Typeset by Vivian Head

Printed by Short Run Press, Exeter, UK

Praise for
Tristan/Yseult

'Harry Bonelle's new version taps into the dark and
furious energy of the old saga, surging and juddering
with life. Bonelle's actor's training has encouraged him
to liberate the performance piece that its original author
must have intended. Thrilling on the page,
but even more so spoken loud.'

SIMON CALLOW

*　　*　　*

'Bonelle's authentically original reimagining is
vibrantly alive through his extraordinary use of language.
I was entirely drawn in to his inventiveness and immersed
in each moment of his vision. He takes you on a journey
of sound, light and emotional punch. Truly a new
voice to be celebrated!'

ARMEN GREGORY

*　　*　　*

'In this reimagining of the Tristan and Yseult myth,
Harry Bonelle uses taut and timeless language and strong
imagery to craft an atmospheric and challenging poem,
that melds the lyrical and the violent to powerful and
memorable effect. Innovative and haunting by turns,
it is full of surprise and originality.'

ANGUS GRAHAM-CAMPBELL

Contents

Preface

The legend of Tristan and Yseult is ripe for retelling. In its many incarnations we find the archetypes of the orphan prince; the highborn sorceress; the warrior giant; the feeble king; and of course, the lovers from two rival factions. Themes of the struggle of the human condition abound, with loyalty, honour and duty set sharply against erotic desire and the yearning for transcendence.

Over the centuries, certain episodes of the legend have proved especially popular with its various narrators. However, rather than relating the drinking of the love potion or the secret affair under King Mark's nose, this poem covers an earlier episode. We open on a Tristan without an Yseult, and close on an Yseult without a Tristan. The narrative defies proper syntax and gives rise to many unresolved mysteries, but the plot is straightforward: a prince duels a giant; the prince wins, but is poisoned; he drifts across the sea and arrives at a hostile kingdom; a princess rescues and heals him in secret; their mutual desire ignites; she discovers his true identity; she tries to kill him but cannot; he vanishes without a trace.

Why choose to retell this episode? It is one of lasts and firsts. It marks a cosmically significant shift from world to world. This is Tristan's last foray as the noble hero cleaving to king and country, and Yseult's last moment of true solitude, existing apart from the war games – and amours – of men. And so, as the constellations declare, they are thrust into their first encounter with the exalted Other, their lives bound forever like a briar on a tombstone. Allegiances wash away, and in that dimly lit bedchamber overlooking an empty sea they seek to transcend the world of things. That this transcendence cannot be fulfilled is the existential full stop on which we end. The stark light of day confronts them; let another world host the consummation of their souls.

My own 'way in' to this Celtic-rooted romance is indebted to Richard Wagner's *Tristan und Isolde*. Just as the sound-world of the opera came to the composer before his libretto or 'poem' did, so the idea for my poem began with the lurches, pleadings, swells and surrenderings of the orchestral score. Not least among the fruits of this inspiration is my use of repeating phrases. They not only repeat, but shift with each repetition, gathering new meaning each time and projecting it back and forward through the text. This is my own verbal take on the musical leitmotifs that have come to distinguish Wagner's composition. There is also a strongly modernist flavour to this poem, and I would be remiss not to credit the influence of T.S. Eliot, James Joyce, Samuel Beckett and Christopher Logue, as well as the medieval sources of the legend.

A few closing words on stylistic choice, then. The focus of the narrative is direct sensory description. The word 'love' never appears in the text. There is no direct speech, no set metre and no rhyme scheme. From the ambiguity and apparent chaos of the verse, I entrust to the reader the emergence of meaning. May it stir, bubble, rise to the surface, then sink back down to the depths.

Harry Bonelle, 2023

Tristan of the Waves

Two Hills

Lurches quick and lurches long.
Steady course, you oars, you rudder,
Hurry not. Do islands move? Is this the way?
Why splay the canvas, muscles wring,
When waves convey you all the same?
The course is good. Put faith in it.
The destination can't but wait. Two hills.
They are of older things than shell alone.
Haste! Haste!, would be your cry
Were not this so. It doesn't move. It is no shell
Of double hump, and under sleeping
Turtle great who rouses slow in tidal wake.
Were so, haste haste would rightly be, for
Samson's Isle, its low twin hills, would quit its
Spot in salt and sea at whim of Turtle's
Appetite. It would be gone upon his back.

Two hills, and strait connecting them. The strip
Of rock will host their feet. When narrowest,

At highest tide, there will it be. When light falls
Furthest from the sky. When brine is drawn to
Slim the strip. When man's recourse to
Cowardice is trimmed to nil. A strip of rock,
Lit sharp by noon. When shadows grow short,
Tristan cannot hide. The waves convey him.

Riding crest and sinking trough,
From rich Tintagel launched with lurches.
How the bended pine cried out when silent
Shepherds and messengers saw her
Put to sea. Libations poured from royal cups,
Filled with tears of folk. Tribute drink.
Tribute shed. Of flesh must tribute never be.
So Tristan does not hide. He staked his head
For sake of the turbulent. Flocks of youths
Spared servitude. For sake of them, this one,
This prince among them staked his
Fate and theirs. He does not hide at peaks or
Depths. When deep the hull is towed,
He keeps his head high as shipmates
Cower in the shadow. For when one billow
Drags us low, another must bear us up.
Highest, then, exalted in day, is Tristan
When the prow is up, and pointing to the sun.

A shame to shrink when our vessels sink low
In shade. For when they rise again,
Our eyes are shuttered still.

His head is high as up they climb.
And so is he first to spy the island.
Cresting waves show new horizons.
There the fight will be. Their course is
Strong as the enemy. Those shoulders
Outmuscle the Nazirite's. Two hills
Come heaving, old and low. Ho, steersman!
Samson rears its back.

And furl. No further. Not for them.
The Cornishmen weigh anchor. Yes my prince.
Right here my prince. And you right there,
Right there my prince. The Cornish ship sits.
She doesn't move. His armour, men. His arms,
Take care. No point in haste. The enemy watch
Upon the shore. You watch the enemy from
The waves, conveyed but up and down with
Anchor weighed. He's ready now. They watch
Their tribute from the shore. Good sport, and
Better trophies. Such the Morholt's thoughts.
His tribute decanted from royal vessel

into a paddle boat? Sport! What sport!
A prince? A vassal, foundling-boy.
The champion of his vassal-land. The gall,
What gall, as anchor is hoisted.
The Cornish unfurl and are turning back.
A prince and his paddle, then. Tribute of one.
His head will do. And Ireland will take its pay
From the dead. If this the way, go on lads! Go!
But leave The Morholt his paddle boat too.
Those shoulders can row to haven back.

So Irishmen gather their anchor too.
Their sails are purple as north they tack.
No champion hides. He fights in the light,
Behind the back of none.
The giant rises against the sun.

Comes Tristan the prince
In his day-dappled boat.

The giant, the Morholt, waits
Where two hills meet.

On Samson's Isle

A tide-tongue slavers its salt ashore. The boat
Comes with it. Swish the shale and split it too.
The hull's aground. A crackle. Stop. The wave
Recedes, and leaves its haul. Step one, step
Two, his boots find land that parts below.
Heel toe, keep crunching, stop. A thought.
Observing him, brute? Your beard-bristles red,
Stretching and sharp? Your arms as bolts
Pulled shut on the lock of your heart?
Unfold, dread Morholt. Slack that grin.
Your enemy pivots, toe heel on hull, and
Launches her back. Let barnacles harvest his
Paddle boat. At Tristan's kick, his craft cuts up
The coming tide. Her struggle is short.
She founders out to a deeper spot, and offers
Her belly to God. The pine turns polyp turns
Nothing at all. Sunk to sea bed. For one,
One vessel lone, will be needed when duel is
Done. For only one champion of the Celts
May be. But one. So one alone may leave
This isle. Your prince has spoken.

What? Speak up.

Have done. Have at. So Tristan draws. In all
The world, no other thing made purely to kill
A man. The spear for deer, a sling for
Stunning, arrows for scattering crows from
Carrion, pick for tunnelling, hook for worms,
And the knife for parting pearl from tripe –
Once something bites. But these are not
The sword. The sword was born to kill a man.

And is its mark a man? You know better,
Princeling. Think. Lurch and lunge
As well you may, you'd be lucky to crop the
Morholt's beard. He's bristling, Tristan. Noon.
Sun high. His pate scrapes the sky-wake that
Filters its light. Drawn and ready
As well you may be, a giant waits.

And giants are slow. Haste. Haste!
For king and Kernow, prince! Well-booted you,
Make shallow in shale those closening prints.
Swift skim pebble launched skip rock skip
Wave like a stone split the eye of the
Philistine. You are that stone!

Your skill that sling! And slung by God Himself.
And what stuns may kill, Tristan. Yes.
Even if not its Creator's will.

Grip gripped double, blade up and right.
High tide. Long light. Step one, step two three
Four step stride. The strait is slimmed
On Samson's Isle. No shade cast. Noontide.
Fight.
Princely visor shut and set. Eight step
Crunch ten closening. The pebbled isthmus
Narrowest. Two hills and strip.
Thyroid on the Cornish throat.
Checked step. Twelve and stagger next –
The giant, scared? To boat turned back?
Is this surrender, Éire's shame? Reaching in.
His skin-shoes lapped. Tristan, stop.
What sport's afoot? The searchings of
A split in time – too short to warn.
Waves silent break. So Tristan steps.

Twelve and a half.

Crunch.

Domi Duellique

The enemy quick. Fibres fired, organ hot.
Fingertip launched. Backhand arc with
Osprey eye. The giant's prize as first strike
Lands. No thirteenth print for prince's push.
Tristan stopped. Tristan stung. Of sharpened
Bone the buried barb, where spaulder leaves
Bare the brace-join.

The slinger smirks red. Sees tribute see
What's stopped his jug. No blood.
The bone-barb nestled. At home.
No pain. Numb numb. Try rolling it. Yes,
Your left is fine as right that wields the sword.
Well slung, dread Morholt. Cowards clap you.
He'll keep the cork nice and snug,
Don't mind him. No, don't mind as
Cornwall lifts its chin. No don't mind him.
Those unshuttered eyes on you on you that
Spy anew the low twin hills just heaving to be
Hewn. In half. Where trap meets neck.
Yes, that's it. Right there, right there you
Prince. Split it.

Up and right, right round grip,
Left palm pommel, point to sun and
Edges east and westwards shift.
Split shale with sole. Step step count steps
Count strides unstopped. Crunches shallower.
Higher pitch swift. Smirking slacks and pebble
Skims, tip approach, tidal breath inhaling
Death and time past high for Ireland's might.
The Morholt roars. Brings the axe. Behind his
Hide-clad back it hid – now splits its sheath at
The drawing. Never mind. The giant's wife
Can stitch it once he's home.

Once they're wed. And she's suffered for
Sharping so poor a bone.

Tristan rushing. No stone unrolled. No check
Now now it's here too close. The Morholt
Plants a heel, dips right, arcs low to high
With his hand-axe flat. Scoop and launch.
Shale flies from giant to man. Man clank
Clank. Pebble-dashed and blinded.
Tiny enemies in the hale sent horizontally
Visor-grille. Shut your eyes. They are no good.
Not when a giant looms too close and lifts the

Axe and bristles grin and dead to light.

Trust other organs. Older things.
Be sense itself in death's grey shade.
What do the waves tell you, lad?

This. Knee drop. He's doing it. Spit grit.
Keep on. Grim faith. He's doing it watch now
Elbows back. Left palm pommel, pivots blade
On plane direct. Right fist grip.
Crouching prince and his sword tip.
Elbow lock. To home. Thrust.

Staunch

Silence of split. Something has been done.
No sun, no sky sea sand-worm interrupts.
Two hills alone see tide go past the peak.
A cloud grows big and grows.

Tristan is not dead. To ask how
Would be luxury. Save it. For now is
Scramble back get back make space from
What you've done put stone in sling back there
And blink and GET this helmet off.

Comes off and clog falls out. Shale to strip
Returned. Cough and clear, blink. Breathe.
And see what you have done. Has that?..
What's red and runs along the ground,
His tip and the Morholt's thigh hot-threaded?
Cannot tell you how bright it is. It flows and it
Shifts and the spilled is all at sea. He dropped
His axe as soon as stabbed. Now he moans.

One moan no more. At halt full stopped.
Femoral split. The giant's axe sits

For scholars to find. Two hands to thigh just
Stop it coming out but they can't. So huge and
Pinprick small but they can't Morholt can they?
No moan no roar is any good. Please, Tristan.
Eyes on you. Draining heart on you on you and
Crunch to knees. His organs drop.
And you just sit and watch. Your work
Unstitched what God has sewn. It's wrong.

That what's inside spills out is wrong.
Red flow red froth. The Morholt crouched tight
Hands in lap. More good in prayer than trying
To staunch. Too late for all but mercy, lord just
Stop it princeling help. Two wrongs
Can right it. Take the sword and finish the job.
Cornwall's tribute. Praise Him.

Morholt pooling. Tristan comes.
His sword in hand retraces that red line.
Needle follows thread reverse. Mercy, man.
Undo, and do. The crunch stop measure up.
Eye-eye man stand to giant crouched.
So bright his face exsanguinated.
Never so white the Irish cheek.
A perfect canvas blesses its paint.

That green eye bright and haloed blue bright
Blue and blackest night. Cosmic spirals
Shrunk to size. Two hearts drained black.
Too bright to tell. Galaxies with heart of void.
And beautiful let them be. Swing blade back

~~DERDERDER~~

Red right to left. Right there you prince.
And pretty too. Brushstroke bold
As ancient ink. Parchment parts at
Anointment. Split. Temple curtain torn in two.
Orbital cracked. Mortal veil no more. In tears.
And red bursts bright through Morholt's head.
Can he tell? Does he know what
Man has done? The tide goes out.

Two Shards

It's done. He crouches there it's done.
Sword in head. Left eye dead edge deep
Embedded. Right eye leftwards to assess.
Giant hands grope at the blade. Get it out.
Any moment now he'll fade.
So Tristan waits two hands on grip and
Watching watching surely now? Or now?
Must have been the kill.

No. Not done. Enough of Morholt clings,
And will till out it slides and back in sheath
And spirit back to stone below.
But bodies are made of such as this.
So Tristan pulls and it's not enough.
Blue lips wince, no more. Again. Harder now
And a grunt this time. Side-split head lurch
With the blade. Right eye on him. Stuck still.
And is that all? Extract. It isn't stone.
Just bone and softer things. Pathetic.

Morholt's smile that makes him stop.
Princeling steps back two three hands off.

Let him show you how it's done.
Pommel pointing. Tip behind. Edge in head.
The giant rises slow. Point to prove.
Now watch.
He stands, scarce liquid left to weep
From head, from leg, to warm the ground.
Grimace still. Eye on you. And giant hands
Around your blade and one thrust. One.
One thrust away and clatter down. That's how.
And giant's bright eye rolls to brain and down
He topples. One crunch loud.
White lips smile in silent prayer.
The sword will never be the same.

Death takes its trophy. Tribute claimed.
Conqueror wins. Sword-shard nestles in
Conquered head. The prize is his.

So now he's dead it's what you did. Dead now.
Still and smiling. Cornwall's time now raid and
Claim them. North necks white in yokes.
Only spared for use. Smile Morholt.
Free most of all. Lie there drain there dead
Eyes shut. Never the woman to
Lock them open.

Mercy, mercy. Praise the night.
Day-slave Tristan sheaths his sword.
Cracked edge catches scabbard. In.
Last look corpse. Nothing. Cold sky.
No wind blows. And still and heard cries from
Within. One bone too many in him.
It is woman's. So extract.
Give her will some manifest.

Finger thumb so easy pull. Easy slide out
BRIGHTEST white in BURST on burst.
Bone-shard's art is in delay. Tristan's eyes
Beaming white pop dazzled. Drops the bone.
Hot tip red and green veined artful. Crafted to
Harm by degrees. Bit bit.

No witness sees what Tristan is
Driven to next. A step. Another step eyes
Sharp white so alive as body fades lurch to
Paddle boat crunches mute ear drums death
Coming deaden step step sinking shaking
Hands gather shale up wooden on hull touch
Brim grip rollock and push please push it
Catch up to tide goes out, shadows of
Strength, spend them lest the white light win.

Tristan pushes the boat to sea. It floats.
He falls within. The paddle is not used.
His course is of the waves. They take him.
Eyes' white light goes out, and so the tide the
Tide the waves the grey sky tide the waves
And waves and waves and

*   *   *

Wake.

Stars and star shapes. Open night.
Cast in silver faint and far.
There the hunter, hounds and prey.
Chase burns on through blink and stare.
Three points three belt studs crown flanked
Bright either side by kings. Anguish north and
Mark the southern. Mark amidst
The prince in darkness. Fastened belt his
Shoulder pads glint, middle one's hand,
Warrior eye on you small boat.
Sky's middle hunter could paddle her home,
Were not his hand with sword. Were not
His shield on two horns set. No help.
The dog must crop the hare. Jaw-stars
Sharped on bone. His great white canine
Sears the night biting days too long
Of tooth and life. It will be over soon.
No brighter thing the sky splays.
Starlight in the wake. No shore no tide.
Listen to oblivion's lap. What comes and
Comes and come it must, receding
Back to deep. Unwake.

*　　*　　*

Clouds have settled from the east.
Dark on deck. Day waits yet.
Who wakes wakes blind to cosmic light.
Yet star beams bless the ones who dream
Dream on them. Back. No clouds in sleep.
Its blackness clear. Sink back then.
Dream-stars greet the dying.
Void and bare the air.

*　　*　　*

Drifts in and round the cochlea around and
Down its spiral sinks to rouse the senses
From the numb. First it breathes, sounding
None, salted breeze, calling dumb as it comes,
Then gives voice, planet's lungs, pipe and
Valve, all blow and it grows, high winds call,
High seas churn, sun splits through, hull
Towed organs lurch, fearing day, blaring
Squall, all stops pulled away, God forsakes,
Cruel His hand, hurled on waves, faith
Sunk to the sand, then finish your battle

Tristan give your body to brine and cresting,
No pity divine to lament what is
Death-marked and already dead

                    *
                        *
                              *

the stop didn't come. Storms fade.
Fainted and floating on.
Did you think it would that easy? Sleep.

                  *   *   *

Starlit shrouded starlit shrouded starlit.
Lids lift still alive. Night and violence.
Elements fight. Clouded cleared out clouded.
The winds the winds the currents and
Closening. It is getting close.
Pulled along lurch along tipping tip
Press press flat hold on. Northening.
Mapped by its star. Lit black lit black.

Cloud rush cover show over off.
                    Sick.
Uncovered for a moment.
Eye slip down the pole down to
Her. Bearing sheaves of it her cure. She.
And he dotes on her on her
Already in soul turn eyes turn heart.
Turn trickle away. Virgin of the bones.
Her stars are skeleton. Sharp stop.
Moments turn. This one turns. Wheat is
Cropped. Dark blind. Closing lids and
Closed now lurch lurch but a peace in
Bound to die. Maid white in spots
By charters tethered shape enclosed and
Burned on cornea. Purer fire.
Cannot speak nor needn't. How it is
Is white and how it feels as waves and
Waking death.

                *   *   *

Sound back. Welcome. Breeze on it calling.
Gulls rock nesting. Haven blue is all it is.

Not a cloud. Birds circle light.
Sky salt daylight back. Your boat. You.
Lap bow to lap. Louder as it
Comes.

Waking Yseult

Whitehaven

The white stone is Whitehaven, the black
Tintagel. King Anguish of Ireland demands
tribute from Cornwall. Three hundred youths
and three hundred maids must be chosen by
lot and delivered each year. For fifteen years
King Mark of Cornwall has flouted this
custom. He is to surrender his kingdom and
his people. The white pebbles are the Irish
ships. They are mustering along Ireland's
eastern coast. When the champion comes
home, the beacons are to be lit. The red beads
are the beacons. The white pebbles are moved
to Cornwall's northern coast. The black stone
is removed. A new white stone replaces the
black stone.

Island realm port castle war room.
Stifling out to in.
Corner always the same stand in.

Father and mother demand it.
All to see petty blocks petty marks and to
Shudder as scraped across hide.
Three calves died for this.
Flayed and made a great big map.
Skin stretch again but over oak top now and
Adorned with scratch scratch feather tip
Dripping and set. Pretty work.
Purpose death in death to serve.

Father Anguish mother Yseult.
Name from mother. State from him.
For there among the pebbles white stone
Black south of red beads in the sea
Two blocks touch outsize their isle
In the sea. One is he.
Why is he not back?

King coughs king king. Walls are salt wet.
Queen Yseult attends. The men in metal rattle
On and what we'll do to break them
And they scrape their toys on painted skin
As if their blades on Brittonics.
But he is not back.

Corners work. For her.
Ghost king ailing queen attending
Rattle rattle prattle tattle
No one sees her scrape her back
Along the salt to edge
To peter out and slip.

Corridor carpet on for a bit.
Turns about then up a step.
Handle turn. In. Stifled do it
Quick swap royal furs for hood and
Out swing frame shut down
Quicker out turn rugs draped sconce
Leave this just be

Out. The fish door. Where the finest hauls.
Salty stone is slick and porous hard hard
Loud and out. Gut-sounds of the sea.
Churns breaks breathing swell.
Gull cry diving sweepers.
She is filled. Salt and living.
It's as if no seat of hers is
Castling at her back.

Little cobbled bits go down
The battlements as jut teeth in the
Grout-gum. This is what she likes.
Step horizon step rock coast step
Harbour back perches step sigh
A slipper two slippers on tide swept beach
Nothing for breathing for anywhere
Yseult alone for the last time. In the waves.

Listens echo back nothing sea nothing air
Silent sweet for last time. Savour it.

Savour it.

Ant

New rust. The teeth don't lie.
Something on her beach that hasn't
Years in all years hasn't been.
Sweep tide's out all manner of things
Dot dots beam dead flesh dark matter
Old things but not this. Go to it.
She makes that hood a habit. Tight wrap.
Yseult of Whitehaven Fair Yseult
Was left with her fur cloak in chambers.
Now she is a tight cowl carrying ears and
Tongue teeth nostrils goosebump
Eyes. Carried on a frame that two feet carry
To what keeps worse her toothache.

Grit. Round an outcrop barren stretch
But there upon the slim strip haven
A turtle on its back and ants devouring.
How they scratch the wooden shell.
And how the metal belly bloats with grey light
DO NOT TOUCH HIM.

Ants' eyes stare and ant hands quiver.

Thorax thin one two three four the
Five of them will carry him.

She does not know if she wants it to be him.
He was not good to her.

The ant men see her mark this fear her.
Lowly lives are made self-knowing
In the shade of such as close
She's close now lads.
Her hood's missing its lining.
Does she think that she can hide?

Scatter from carapace gather your rags.
Await instruction from the tongue.
Tang unbearable now.
Peel the rust husk bag it up yes
Flog it in port if you must just do.
And it is done and as the ants strip
Scale and plate from what's washed in
The grey light parts and white too white
And cannot see the sickness in him
For she cannot tell for it is now
The only thing. And she is not alone.
And she is no more I nor she no
There is only and.

Secretion

It must have happened wordlessly.
Five in a train white flesh aloft
Bags clank clank dragged along.
Ant men two a side nestwards lift
And Yseult the adamant with her hands.
Hilt and pad and fingertip on him on his
Salt skin his kelped hair. Lock step.
They take the washed up feet first bedwards,
She at the back at his head
To keep his facing the grey sun.

Haste. The council can't have much
To scratch in record scrape on skin.
Get him in and nestled.
His smell should be yes something else
But it is so like home.
So haste up struggle step tramp enamel
Up to throat to fish door threshold.

In relief. King queen voices echo statesmen
Still shut in the war room.
Revenants not yet in breach of tomb.

Eight soles nake wool slippers twin bind
Stone to carpet. Shuffle and static.
Footsteps keep the torches lit
All long the corridors.

Closen clank that could betray but she
On him the world within her basin.
Stare into the deep as false light
Flickers first time on and in her eyes.
And all of him is leaking him and
Fire draws the deepen up.

Flickers off congeal again and back
Stop. Maid to chambers. Where's Brangenn?
Ants to anthills. No no pickings
Shouldn't be here so you're simply sent.
Your pay will be the story.

Trail of salt sand grit sea smell
Ends at Yseult's little door.
Turn handle in and gentle heave bags in
And where can Brangenn but she mustn't.
If she leaves him he could melt between
The pavings fibres glass frames.
He unshelled soft urgent in pull,

Two bare feet slide past the frame.

Door is shut by raw desire
And they are in that world is theirs.
All that leaks in atrium can spill and hot burst
In that world that seals the stuff.
She is not alone Yseult
On chamber floor some
Where between the fur and older things.
Dark hair spills grip one with fibres
One with other one with one fix point
But he is dying. She is made to live.

Enough of this.

What She Does

His sword and armour sit in the
Beach urchins' bags. She shoves them in the
Corner with a blooded strength.
She shifts the dying man
Onto the rug and straightens him.
His sickness curdles where it sits a tiny well.
He is not so hard to move.

She removes his clothes and underclothes
And lights a candle brings it close.
Calluses, salt crust, wind fray white lips
What she sees
Yet couldn't vein him green like this.
Until by touch as well as wax light
She perceives that small intrusion
Where his shoulder joins his breast.
As if was stitched at needlepoint,
Sewn together with holy seams
Until the Artist found the thread
Was not enough. Had to be
Snapped before that join stitched shut.
An open wound upon His work.

Malspore? Crushed, mixed with Torricite...
No, with Lady's Fate. Or Drakefork?
It has festered in the winds.
The waves have brought the sea in. Good.
Salt in a wound as this can
Check poison's course.

She brings herself back from his heart.
Bends and ear and back. It beats
Like a prisoner's drum in there.
Brings an ear to two white lips.
Ghost of a breath shift out shift in.

Good.

Morley Milk and Sipleaf. Goursel for the sores.

Up she up to cabinet swing slide
Fingers run on rim cork rim cork.
Balsam for burns, docks for stinging,
Spirits for purifying and pain,
And Deathdraught to end it.
But these are not the healer's needs.
She bearing pestle Morley milks and
Gathers in mortar. Leaves in

Sip it soak grow again.
Sponges green and sponges black.
Sage Yseult her art on him her work.

Down grind side stain speckle the pestle and
Dip tilt sticking and in. Needs heat.
Turn back to him that brightest thing
But dim and dim as deadened wick set by him.
She had not noticed it go out.
Their chamber world that
No place not for light.

The remedy needs heat so suffer firelight
Till he wakes. Then their place
Dim and rich again.
So Yseult to door to get the torch in corridor
And open slipper hem woven up girdle
Heart of a statue. True friend beautiful.
She is here.
Brangenn she says Brangenn Yseult.
Maidservant so so serve and
Lift the torch from sconce.
In if you promise not to scream.

Ever obedient. Good Brangenn.

In and what have you done
In vacuum of her mouth.
What words there might have been burned up
As flicker shine on him as God intended.
Questions later. What they do now.

Thatchings lit under crucible. Solution poured
Solution warmed. Bubble one and done.
Yseult and Brangenn. Torch bearer present
Tries not to question her mistress
Simply light. Her lady kneels at sickness side.
Two pairs two lips part. In.
Laps of white specks green black neutral
Fill the emptied spaces. Vein save.
She at his head to tilt and guide as
Remedy waves down his red.

Her maid cannot and must she does.
The sheets are in the cupboard, mistress.
Is she in that world?
Brangenn the out look in retrieves.
Single hand drapes place right there yes
Over him. The shames of day folk
Flocked and hived. He and she are else.
Had not occurred.

To bowl silt all gone down.
In there it beats measure stable made good.
To yellow hence bluer his blood already.
Ah, Yseult. Art from mother.
Shame from servant.

Man is naked. Remedy. Brangenn you are to
Wash him. Up. Her lady up to window.
You her friend that bucket half full fresh yet.
The flannel is on the side. Your hands please.
Yes and put out that flame. Something new
Not good bad no but new and every so
Put out that flame as Yseult the grey sky
Looking out the void sea look out
Not to turn and watch what maid is to
Wash press rub.

Sound is magic enough.

Blue Mind

Fabric and shutters unshuttered and freed.
Her people's sea. Saviour's sky.
Pure bone speckles and star spots hide.
Virgin wakes her art by night.

Stone shell blue in broad cloud strokes
So wide to fill an Irish eye.
Blend and filter to the salt that
Buoys no man not holds his back.

Scraping waves bring no old triumph.
And so does she know the fate of Ireland
Ere the rattlers with their maps.
No more told no with red barb red hand.

Sheet is off that sweep sounds sweet.
Tongue touch palette wet him suck
The salt specks sponge. Obedient maid.
Lady Yseult disobeys her gut and
Stays and stares no turning bare eye
On that blue deep grey high blend.
Bucket and plunge drink up and squeeze.

A trickle. Three. Salt dissolves.
Soon the bare one smooth prepared.
Rippled and waved the plane she sees.

Where to press the Goursel mistress where
Wherever the body flames. Good.
Brangenn is fetching wetting pressing her
Warmth through the lattice to source.

Bowing sores red hills stop heaving.
A billow to north is ridden by lap white
As her haul unhusked is dried.
What the sage will find inside him.

Stoic Yseult. Her neck stays stone.
Her sockets marble carved. Eyes hard.
Lapis lazuli the mind as sky salt surges
Sea around it shifted eastwards in and west.
Dress him. Linen cupboard. Stitched and
Pressed for the Morholt so.

They'll be a little big.

Blick

Look linings cuffs. Swatches seams.
Soft on softer white covers whiter.
Squat slide forearms. Look at him.
Four hands take care and
Lift. Lighter than what he ought.
The rug will dry.

In blanket over tucked in cover.
Safe serene a pilgrim's sleep.
Now she and he alone, Brangenn. Be good.

Lady food care secrecy what then?
Tell council taken ill caught chill.
They will well rash then over throat and
Creeping head and breastwards red.

Lady Yseult is not to be seen.

Brangenn her patient go between.

Brow bow very well hinge pad out locks pad
Breathe, breathe, tide and sink and swell,

Slow, ease no only
Be, hurts, no hurts, mood in mood on

Him. Blazing in the dim.

She sees now how white has all colours in.
Fawn swift mane oak top root riverbank
Rose beach stone afternoon clouds petal prim
Pebble new bone eggshell wet sky orbit
Mint in fade field layer fog faint valley
Red. And all in shape and shade and hair vein
Flesh.

Hid and lure the pair.

Sleeping waking waves apart.
Lap trickle lap still surge over swell lurch.
One to balance the waves of other one
So to be the same one one.

Sun lowering. Let the dim be theirs
Be shared a gaze for glance untainted
By a castle candle flame. Keep blaze away.
Seagull passes circles back eye bead
Gold black to sleeper drawn, and the sage

Attending all in still on them on them.

Bird perches salt on sill. Shakes the spray
From feather tips. Talon stick
And yellow strong
Unblink and bid the lens the need.

Yseult the purer fair man's curer from her
White blaze looks and looks
To clear keen gaze. Which stiller, gull maid
A happening here
About to brought to light.

The seagull blinks.

All wing it spreads apart the bill and
R ENDS the silence shrill and now.
Sill departs. Back to brine top.
Fate call done the ones' alarm.
So she to him enshrined her glance.
And his to hers at last.
He is awake. Her waking fate.
And what she sees is death.

And

The Sealing

Drink. Filled and savour prince. There right
As one in the dim two looks meet as
Two parts returned from the deepening close.
Where are you and how?
The clusters bow for what you see.
Shattering stars between the
Eyes of His that given light.
Dilate. Obedient eye. Drink in in dim.
What amber his and powder hers
By black sea bed and spreading. In to out.
And only one can break while two souls still.

It's you? What will, what will you one.
Yes only up and tresswards glint.
Each work of His deserves its frame.
Gilded glide. Tumble hold.
Flax and wheat she fair.
Princeling thank the dim.
Else she too white to see.

Blood beholder. Is he back?
Good Yseult her brewing skill
Revives the sick vein back to waves.
The waves that lift him under scrub skin.

Water got. Water in. Of gritless water
Washed up slaked. Spun fabric sits its soft
On him. Its warm reward. She hold.
Cup warmed at rim.
Fingertips take their share from there.

Last sun to trim the dim.
It's yours. Keep day-flame far.
Where torches seal let blood instead.

Fragments

They must have spoken finally.
Whatever spoken something sure.
For course of days and short short nights
The healer and her haul are bound.
He aground in cushioning.
She a chamber pad attends.
But the spoken only cup wash look
And swell down warmer green well drained.
There are no reasons for their names.
Only float so far from alone
And hold the one blood in the hearts.
A night it's night and silent speaks.

She wakes and never slept.
She is waking. Ever look and ever by.
Wet wovens or a broth.

At high sun gulls cry. Silence split
The head the head the curtain draw
Lest torn in two when must be one.
Yseult wind silk. Each temple bound.
The writhing man and his ears wound over.

Soothes him. Sleep to last him.
She must wake stay feed desire.

Sat nigh as he breathes, expands, is and
Dreams, no dreamer she and watches
Settling dusk. Maidservant calls.
Grain berry milk bearing.
Not much longer, mistress. Days and nights.
Lock on the edge of your door so much
Can hold. Have thanks away.
The man is healing.

Pieces back of him of him seal back in place
Where chooses she.
The whole the two the one two.
Peace. Will you break it? Not enough to stir,
Yseult. Only see, and touch it too.
No eye on you wan you with candle wax
Refused. Ward former clads sharp.
Check they're there.
The corner where you left them bagged.
Open in. Have care the edges but
Glory skim the work is fine! She's seen
Her share on the war room rattlers.
Even bagged and manless she can tell.

Something else. In there the not to clad,
To kill. A beam-straight serpent, flat and made
To kill a man. To thrill a maid as
Scabbard in sleep. Lady of the land of Éire,
Lift and draw. Little song of steel and
Tempered things. His will in hilt where sits
Its beauty plain, its brutal nature
Honed to slick swish sweet.
But this is odd. A piece is missing. Jagged gap
In edge. To scabbard back bag.
He'll need his nighttime cup. He stirs.

You're in and out, man, each time out
You're strengthening. More the balms
Or hands that do the balming? Shame to
Sweat at the touch of a palm such.
Be better when the sun downs.

Waking undered wake it under
How many days and nights?
She knows. So settle, man. What? Speak up.

What He Says

How many days and how many nights?
Two of each since waking and today.
He sounds just as and she not at all now
Back to older ways of being with another one.
The tide is in. Breaks against the stairs
Beneath the fish door. Paddle boat barnacled
Gone drift now.

What sea what land? The Irish Ireland
Her sea her seat. Well enough better breathe
Better speak NAME yourself how so.
Brittonic to Goidelic Éire to Kernow
Man to woman and to and
One stands in grey light one sits up
In sweet shade says that

Tantris. Nomad. No man so alone. To begin.
Brittany weaned and Mann raised.
Mark Tantris' anguish at Lesnewth, its rock
Tintagel that launched with urchin pirates
Manned the ship boarded his in the Biscay.
On his way to Galician parts

To learn to read the stars.
Tantris knows the Goat Fish west,
The eastern Bird of Flame and
North Bear. Southwards Horse Man
Known to Tantris too.
And pinned and pining wheatsheaf
Virgin of his bones.
This one's in the middle.
Yet these no heaven make alone so
Tantris braved the waves alone along
All along the Celtic coasts.
Oh and he can fight and
Pitched his best against
The Cornish marauders boarded her.
Her name herself the Triskelion, dame.
Tantris trusts her hull prow salvaged.
So King Mark's raiders licked him, yes,
With crafty barb and poisoning.
Tantris took their heads, fear not.
Then others came. He paddled ailed and nights
Blinked out the stars. Till now.

Now Tantris cannot blink away.
All other lights offend.

Yseult. You close died closening but
What she did.

Know her name and flatter prattle
Back to Mann.

That Night

That night she seals the cap on her healing.
Art is good. From mother learned. All while
Brave Tantris pillowed sits and
Eyes on them the stars.
There's the Hare like a lattice a fleeting in
Flight. Lurches short. Why fly the night,
Leaving little pad little prints
All across the sky? It's not by choice, Yseult.
Hare is hounded by
Goursel more. Wet and warm.
She wipes the raised and silvering
When starlit. Press. Beats firm. Bettering.

The Big Dog savour it. This won't be
Every night. He lunges close to crop a heel,
Topped by brighter bright. Hot searer.
Fang of older things than
Eyes which mirror back the shards in out and
In an Irish eye. His turned to
Side hers on on his. Sip Morley.

Trained upon the Hunter even as he sips.

Swallows and carapace, shielded studs
One two and he the middle one.
So sharp. All bone and temper.
Water washes green down red.
All settled she cups his head down rest
Palm soothe lock tumble slow and soft weigh.

Man from Mann gives window ear and eye
Yseult to meet in dwindle starlight shroud.
Clouds closening. Rains cover all.
Two shapes. Two wills. In darkness find
Their one. One thigh linen padding skirts thigh.
Warm tether. She sits. What is stitching
What together. Close one close.
And still and stir. Perfume antidote pulse rose
And rising without moving. Wake.
Breathing wave wake wave recede,
Sea change in the organs hot.
Body salt bloods flowing things and
One and and what she does now

She stands. Your vigil keep, secreter.
Sleep is for the dead.

He sleeps.

*   *   *

head home

thunk seagulls shitting in the sky get up wait
nothing works get up no shit i see and hear
but thats about it who are you no stop what
are you doing im moving upright god im low
im a giant whats this oh poor fucker lying
there you lost alright so wait those skin boots
breeches fur wraps tunic those are mine hes
huge this headless sod i turn two ugly fucks
theyre smirking how is he holding me unless
god no yes im my head a dead head thunked
off floating in his grip so this is what its like
the sea fuck i remember samsons isle the
fight with that little squit i lost it then put me
in where i drop all dark in here and shut in
wait you cornish bastards where are we going
dont leave the rest of me shit here we go yes
there are the ship creaks this will take a while
im bobbing sounds like im on board
somewhere down i go the hold i bet im in the
hold with the shit i swear if this box is cheap
pine and the rats get to me ill have my
revenge were off its all creak thunk thick

swishes all the way thered better be no rat
squeaks bastards well there arent im not in
utter shit then so thats it for ages and ages
and ages and ages and ages and ages and
ages and ages and ages and ages and ages
land ahoy i hear ha cornish talk can go and
hang no beauty of my people none some
bustle bored now oh was that the hatch yes up
we go no doubt were at that shithole tintagel
steps on wood deck first then plank sounds
like and wet stone oh its raining im in a box a
head in a box and its raining shut the world up
itll get it my eyes when that lid opens shush is
that my folk it must be pretty tongue and not
just any yes none else its anguish and yseult
the mum to save me take me home to my
bride shell know what to do she could heal the
dead that girl bright fucking bright put it out
and as i thought so many drops i feel nothing
but my eyes have gone blurry that beacons
bright ow but id know it anywhere ha
whitehaven harbour im home lads home yes
some shade wish i could blink hm faces peer
in yes its the morholt so i didnt beat him yes
he got me god its done now dont get all like

that whats that queens giving orders who is
that so blurry and dark its dark that fire
behind fuck but i think brangenn yes just the
maid ha take me to her come on thats it no
dont you can leave the lid open just keep the
rain out dont no dont and of course alright see
you later then thunk.

shit.

*   *   *

Mná Síde

Her eyes are open. Devoted and dry.
To shut them wet them folly for
Her Tantris is at peace. At war
Their two two beats not. Keep that world
As theirs before the sun curse laid
With rising. Tantris and Yseult.

False. And drier still. Her brow
To window sill to pane to the false
Light trying its shallow refractions.
Wax wane feeble flicker her now.

She'll watch for you she'll watch for you
And nothing is seen.
The clouds have come thick
But where moonlight lacks
The flicker to left. Words sift and
Drop from her lips as she knows.

The beacon is lit. The bay's red bead.
From Samson's twin hills
The one has returned,

And there it burns on the harbour.
There in the not yet dawn how it looks
It's like those silent fairy mounds.
They dot like pebbles the valleys to west
Whose flowers white flowers
Are said by the sages to glow a
Bright rich hearty scarlet, yes, but only, Yseult,
Only when the fairies tread the petals.
When they do as so they choose they choose
To dance unseen by any mortal eye.
But you young sage have laid your two.
And so if one should watch the fay folk
On the mound they'll watch you back.
And they will stop their dance and watch and
Turn the petals to ash. Their little grins go
Gaping black and each little piskie is
Not any longer. That is when they scream
They shake the hollows the moors
The ridges the rocks.
Then know the knowers
That death is come.

Rain falls and becomes the waves.

She curtain draws she thrills goes cold

For that flicker rim amber red under seep
Proclaims the giant's return from the deep
With some sad Briton from scalp to clavicle
Torn. In two. Tribute trophy triumph bringing,
Swung by the locks of his pate unblooded.

Can you hear the titan's steps?
Already they crunch pebble wood thunk
Stone split print deep rug sunk
Closening.

And when he finds that world is yours?
That chamber drawn and dimmed for him and
Not him but for him? The wise
Will learn a thing from the dim. For you Yseult
Will meaning new bring scream.

Rain dribble dash lick tap pane.

My lady.
Split.
My lady.
Hers is come.
Yseult.
Her lady of the mound.

All songs and ink dip scratchings
Never could have warned her organs that
Her lady of the mound would
Call so close so soft near warm
On that the other side of her door.

Breathe for he is back. Wed or dead today.
That is what the banshees say so face those
Two tall shoulders great, and the green rage
Mounts them. Seal fate death beam twain.

Your bolt pulled back from the lock
As a beat of your heart. Unsouled,
Brave daughter. Queen Yseult with Anguish
Soon will mourn their princess in the wake.

Crack that hinge and

Pieces and their Place

Open. Wordless. She is here.
Her drawn face beautiful and stark.
Brangenn she is Brangenn and good
Maidservant serves her lady with
A box. White hands slick and clutching as
The not yet dawn drops sit and quiver top
Then off streak streaking back to ground
For torches on the wall to draw back up.

Her part played what's relayed is
Good. The truth's in it. Her lady knows.
She keeps her slippered toes this side,
Receives it slow and blinklessly.
Brangenn may look within no more
That world is just for them.
No eyes no pair may a share take but the
Dead. That place is not for living.

Threshold pushes damp air back back shut.
Sealed again. Brangenn pad pad
How slight swift sorrowing
Out towards the world of day.

Yseult the lady turns to not yet healed
But close and yes asleep still dreaming
May be good breathe weight.
Your healer of the bone must see.
Weighty wood and what's within.
Set it. There. On brewing table by the window
There where beacon edge glows dim
Around the stitch hem on to it.
Her eyes prefer the half light now so
See by it and know and
Pine smooth wet side grip grip
Opens it.

Reek red red white and red reeking foul.
Hair and what's inside on
Drain skin never so shine and dead. White red.
Trophy shines in not quite light.
Locked shut eyes. Right by rigour.
Left by what he did who split it.

Bedding in the brow blood speck
Mane pallor lash lip dead
Metal in the side white red.
Your tools, Yseult. It is no thing
Of old and stitched. It should not be in there.

Loose and see where it should be
Where came it this cold shard.

Cabinet down drawer haste but soft
She'd spare the man the sight.
Clamp out draw quick grip grip open
Bind the steel two sides. Her left hand holds
The head that used to loom and burn as
His both right and left would fix her. Clamp.

Fine work rich wrought little jagged piece
Comes easily. Her hold is good. Yseult's hand
Honed in draw out slow. In doing and undoing.
Shard slick fluid of fallen. Steel unthreads.
The giant's head at the palm of her hand
Brought low and steady. Breathe it out.
As two split parts two spills of His creation
Ireland and her titan more worth hold.
The sages say new learnings outweigh gold.

Mind your head.

Lid back thunk keep the reek in dark she turns
She turns her clamp and what it grips.
Pretty. Speckled red. Left edge keen straight

Right rip snap hard. Splinter sharp and clear.
Her sleeping starsman, were to see,
Would sure say how its shape recasts
The six side Wagoner in the sky.

His secret her place not to sleep.
His rest need hers forbids for
He is what she is. Is all.
Yseult release your tool on table go to
Tantris that sweet word made flesh
Lock organ bone. That's it his heart,
Slow thrumming warm draw, beat and beat
And in its orbit draws her core, twin stars
Stretching voids to voider wider whitest
In and of and soar above the world of things
Old birthing new born dying
You are beautiful.

She watches you prince.
Lucky foundling. Always found.
Closens now to more than watch.
Lids touch. Older things.
What no man split let pieces come to tether.

She he sleeping waking Yseult

His her eyes veiled in flesh so
Hale in longsome languish match and
Out breaths mingling mouth on mouth.
That sweet stop when breath is spent and
Dying all across your lips. Savour death
Enough in taking. In and slow. Nose tips tingle
Closening to fill with each the other the
Two one salt one leaf sip one two.
Septum to his warmish throat one element
One fume one raw and perfect fill one wave.
How it sounds when you one breathe is
How the ocean yearns the moon is how
You sigh to rising come to float in lifeless and.
In out all hang. God in closing gaps
Between you. Cleft and cleave to.
Steady course heave your wars your shudders
Heave ho heave ho leave
All that in the wake and dream as
And. Stitch it. Sew and yearn need knot
The red to red again. What's left but
What you do? What other thing pure thing
No thing left than
Maid to kiss a man

Lurch.

Deathdraw

Make it bright to see. Off off your healing
Thread stretch up to window. Now. Undraw.

Flames and glass. Two each side of pane
One beacon close and on one roar within.

And foreglow far where are no waves where
Deeper plane grey not yet sooner than before
The morning. Star white hung in grey.
East what draws up north what
Spits the stopped rain out.
Harbour light red mound announce their
Light horizon bringer day grey white,
East is north and either false false wills
The two will settle. Purer fire in heart.
Put faith and
Do.

Yseult takes up the sword. She draws.

One two three four five side gap crack
Left edge thrust. Scabbard drop clatter
Find six. Cast your hex cast iron behind.

Grip in right. Extract from clamp hand
Fragment. Shape as whip hand
Drives the stars.

Shard in left held pommel down right.
Hold them up Yseult to home light
Red white left to right in cast glass.
Her will one with two hands what they do they
Move like planets drawn in each one's orbit.
Southern gods for north drawn bodies.

As the primal ray so near day not yet
Breaks their dim her two grips meet.
Perfect fit. The sixth is brought to five.
Man's blade reforged.

Piece in place. Tantris. How she did not know
That false light spreading spilling from his
Lips. More spill. Curse and carving.
Never even been to Mann.

Rage Yseult contained in hot will place
That little grey shape on sill.
Right grip keep. Grip your left now.
Two hands need to heft heave home.

Turn on him on him two blazes on him.
Flicker off dim lit amber red gold
And the shade that shade Yseult
And blade cast on him. She can see
The breath conveyed still spread still
Spread still peace dream what he must be.
Ripples slight and skin soft heartened
Beauty white wound silk and visions.
What they must be. Memories of the future
Hold of homeward ship and king full cups
Clap clap our prince back home our
Young prince from the waves.
We sent the head to haven right there
Back to bride. Let the Irish hang it
On the mantle. Rot it rots with each igniting,
If they have a hearth, that is.
Have they discovered fire yet?
All pleasure snarl and fleets and treaties.
Long Brittonic rods for backs our backs swing
Crack.

The woman casts a greater shade.

Knee sink linen. Dimpling bone on bed.
Thigh tether. Hilt straight in left
Her right hitch up her skirts to measure gap

Straddle swing. Knee mirrors knee with
His as glass. Touch him and you'll shatter.

Bring both grip back. Point to rafters,
Pommel down him as he dreams of
Her who has his lap.
Thin linen. Folds and heat. Two beats.

Point rise high. Scrape the beams that
Flicker flick fire wake.
Deep breath under sheets.
Her breast suspended.
Stars have split within a moment.
Down potential highest nigh one
Word one deed release, and let the world
Draw down the blade to broken break
The warring will. One swing
To end it. Light awaits. Bring day bring fate.
Yseult the Brave. In breathe and
Drive his sword.

Beam break. One. From the farthest wave on
You. First time light on you on you.
Colours birth themselves on you and
Tristan wakes you lady of the dawn
All things that He created.

Riverbank lily steam flow giver sea sage
Wheatsheaf gather grow earth milk heather
Gold gold stream sun cornflower soft powder
Marrow sand hazel night flitter moon bone
White. All in your in what you are of what
You're made.

What has been made against His will
Is hanging still. No man's gaze can meet it.
Tristan's amber. Tristan's will.
His eyes can only on that blue that
Wakes. And what you are
Cannot but be the end.

This is the look the wasteland gives
To spring and summer rains.
Rain to sunlight. Light to dusk.
Dust to billows and pillows to heads.
All the sweeter when it's two.
One bed to bodies and body to food.
Root to water. Daughter to son.
One to two to one two one two one two one
One twoonetwoonetwoonetwooneoneoneone
Twooneonetwoonetwoonetwooneonetwoone

One.

End

The sword falls from her hand. He does not
Watch it clatter to ground he does not hear it.
All she hears is there that world breath.
All he sees is bright transfigured.
She sees it too he hears it too.
Tether tightest. White ray draw.
This is dawn this dusk and every heartbeat
Birth death in the waves. She sinks into him.
Riverbanks give as all is flow.
To settle. Two ones. One two.
It's not as if the two is one
All is one to pierce to soar bound free
To come to drown. Arms gather her.
Down to float and still that look
As eyes and ribs and old old things they draw.
Closest. Cheek breath one. Swells without an
End and tides and little billows drink the well.
Tristan and Yseult and each is and.
Sunken in to other one in weight in
Time space every bit of matter hums
As one inside and in.
The ringing of the stream of things.

High among the stars.
You are the everburn and the black.
You are plunged and plunging heave
Your fires and your waters are all one.
Let them wash away with each breath
Life goes in and out and out.
To sink and rise. Height and gentle.
Depth of cool and warm to founder.
One is and has found the end with
In the other changed and ever one.
Two hearts one. Lids draw down.
Sealed in the end.

She sleeps. She soars away. The stream.

*   *   *

Whitest. Blaring through to eye. There are
No clouds that morning in the port.
The lady is awake.

Yseult the Sage, Yseult the Younger,
Lady of Whitehaven, Éire's future queen
Alone. Rises quickly. Feet to rug and pivoting.

It is the morning. She is in her room. It is
Not a world it is a room. Nothing there that is
Not what she always had.

Tristan's armour in those bags and
Tristan's sword and Tristan's shard and
Morholt's head in that shut box are gone.

The day is bright. He has gone out into it.

Yseult goes to the window and
She looks to sea.

There are no clouds there are no waves.
There is only blue and sound and salt

She keeps the window shut. Her maid

Brangenn begins to knock. Yseult sees hears
Older things.

She sees through the blue the
Fathoms below the vaults above.
Reef and shoal and seashell rock bed.
Stars and star shapes living and dead.

And all she hears is her own breath
As one as one the waves.